CW00818961

Ghosts of the
Forest of Dean

Charles Pyrke and his servant

see page 13

GHOSTS
of the
Forest of Dean

Sue Law

The Forest Bookshop

Published by
Douglas McLean

at

THE FOREST BOOKSHOP

32 Market Place, Coleford, Glos. GL16 8AA

© **S. Law**
1982

ISBN 0 946252 04 1

Printed in Great Britain by
Logos Ltd.

By day, the Forest of Dean is a welcoming place with an enchanting and unique character of its own, but, as evening draws into night, the mysterious Forest takes over and in hushed voices Foresters tell tales of strange happenings and uncanny places . . .

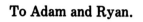
To Adam and Ryan.

THE NAAS GHOST

The ghost of William Morgan, murderer, has been seen haunting Naas Lane. On July 22nd, 1771, William murdered Miss Jones, the youngest daughter of William Jones, Esq. of Naas House, in a meadow near Lydney church as she was walking from Lydney to Naas with a friend. Miss Jones was found lying dead across the path in the meadow, with the back part of her skull beaten, and her friend, a Miss Gough, lay badly injured in a ditch. Every man in the neighbourhood was ordered to go in pursuit of the murderer, and William Morgan, a sawyer, was in bed when neighbours called to tell him of the news. He came downstairs, blood still on his breeches, and confessed to the crime. He said he had been playing 'Fives' on Thursday and gambled away all his money, but had agreed to play for sixpence the next night. Whilst he was worrying over how to acquire the money, the two ladies walked passed him, and he though he could easily rob them as they went home. He followed them, and it being nearly dark, passed them. Miss Jones said, "Goodnight to you, Will". Finding that they knew him, he decided he must murder them, skirted the meadow, came up behind them, and struck Miss Jones to the ground with a stick. Then he dealt her a further blow, which killed her, and chasing after her friend, struck her in the same way. He knelt down and removed Miss Jones' pockets, but left her watch. This is when his breeches became stained with blood. Just then he saw someone approaching with a lantern, and ran off. The pockets which Morgan took from Miss Jones' dress contained a half guinea, five shillings in silver, two pence in copper, and a two-bladed knife. These things were later found in his room, and he was duly tried and convicted for the crime.
Over the years, William's ghost has been seen many times.

A Lydney resident told me of his experience. "I was living at Lydney dock at the time," he said, "and on my way to town one night I saw a tall figure walking in front of me. I dismounted my cycle and got within three yards of this figure, and, as you can imagine, was somewhat taken aback by his attire. He was wearing a stove pipe hat, a khaki coloured cape with a ruffled collar, and thigh boots. It was a cold, very quiet evening, and I was struck by the silence surrounding this man. As he walked I could hear no footsteps, even though he was a big man. I followed him a short way, and just as he reached what was the old mortuary (there are factories there now) he turned to face me. He had long, dark sideburns, a very handsome face, and eyes which were full of sorrow. A terrible feeling of sadness emanated from him. He held my gaze for a few minutes, as if pleading with me to do something, but I could not move. Then abruptly he turned as if to go into the mortuary, but faded away. This was the first time I'd ever seen a ghost and on speaking to an old resident the next day, I was told that the figure had been seen by several people at different times. Then he confessed to me his own ghost story. On a brilliant summer's day he had been strolling down the avenue of lime trees leading to Naas House. Among the thick foliage ahead of him he could see what he thought was a coat blowing in the slight breeze. Walking nearer, it was a body, clothed in a cape and thigh boots, swinging by its neck from a thick rope secured to the tree. He closed his eyes in horror, and when he opened them again the body was not there. I was the first person he'd told about this sighting, and he'd only mentioned it because I'd experienced a similar thing. He made me swear not to tell anyone else, but he is long dead now, so the story can be told. Anyway, this happened to me thirty two years ago, and in those days I didn't mind talking about the ghost, but I soon learnt that people react in all sorts of ways, some of them unkind, to anything to do with the supernatural, so I rarely talk about it now. But I imagine William Morgan still haunts the area. I wonder who has seen him recently?"

Lit by the sun, Naas House looks warm and welcoming. Completed in 1573, it still retains the original carved oak window sills, through, like the rest of the huge house, they are gently crumbling. The lime walk, which stretched from the front of the house to the main road was cut down during the second world war to allow easy access to a prisoner of war camp in the adjoining field. The Biddle family have lived there since 1900, and Michael Biddle says it is almost a losing battle to stop the old place from falling down. "We've never seen a ghost here", he says, "and if there are any, they must be friendly. They've never bothered us."

* * * * * * *

Fifty years ago, Mrs. Trigg of Lydney was walking along a road known as "Back Road". It was a lane thick with bushes, ivy and blackberries. As children, she and her friends always went there to look for the early violets and primroses. It wasn't a busy road. A farm and a couple of cottages were the only buildings there, so it was a very popular walk for the people of Primrose Hill and of other local areas. It was a favourite spot for courting couples, and on this particular dark night, Mrs. Trigg was with a boyfriend. As they strolled along, they became aware of something in the middle of the road. Getting nearer, they saw three figures in long black cloaks, with cowls over their heads. Their monk-like shapes gradually became stronger as she and her friend watched them, frozen to the ground. There was not a sound, and nothing moved. Then fear made them move, and they walked quickly past the monks, looking back only once to discover that they had vanished. The Back Road is now called Driffield Road, and a few private houses have been built there. Today, the road carries a lot of traffic and is much wider; I wonder if it is too busy for the monks now?

* * * * * * *

When Thomas Were, the last Abbot of Flaxely, was forced to lead his monks away from Flaxely Abbey in the days of Henry VIII, one monk, Wulfram, who was eighty years old and stubbornly set in his ways, refused to go. He lived in a secret room in the Abbey, sleeping by day and taking his exercise at night. Up until thirty years ago his ghost, a small bent gray figure, was seen flitting through the meadows and woods around Flaxely at night, as if foraging for food.

* * * * * * *

Littledean
THE MOST HAUNTED VILLAGE

Dean Hall is one of the oldest houses west of the River Severn; there is ample evidence of Roman occupation there, and its name is derived from the Dene family, who were Lords of Dene from 1080 until 1319.

It is the most haunted house in the most haunted village in the Forest and it boasts the only poltergeist of the area. Often, if white flowers are arranged in the dining room they will be flung to the floor, or scattered on the stairs.

For 250 years, the Pyrke family owned the Hall. Over the fireplace in the dining room is a reproduction of an earlier portrait which formerly hung there, of Charles Pyrke and his silver-collared black servant, painted when they were both still boys. In later years, when Charles was twenty three, he was murdered by his servant, who is said to haunt the scene of his crime, both audibly and visibly. Years ago, after the original portrait was taken down, a country scene was put in its place, which repeatedly fell to the ground. In despair of this it was fastened with a chain, but to no avail; it was found on the floor again, this time with the chain broken.

Why Charles Pyrke was murdered is not really known. However, another story tells of a black half-caste baby, murdered and hidden behind the secret panel in the Blue bedroom before his body was disposed of. It seems that the black servant may have had a sister who bore Charles Pyrke's baby, and the baby was hurriedly disposed of, giving the black servant ample motive for murder. In the County Records at the time of Queen Anne there was a report of a "nigger" with a silver collar found straying in the district, who it is thought must have been the guilty man.

Bristol was a centre for the slave trade and not that far

from Littledean, so many of the servants were black slaves. I was told of a fairly recent sighting of a little black boy who patrols the landing outside the Blue bedroom with a candle. About thirty years ago, the Crawley Boevey family lived at Flaxely Abbey. The owner of Dean Hall at that time, Mrs. Corbet Singleton, asked her friend Lady Crawley Boevey if she would like to stay for the weekend. The following morning Mrs. Corbet Singleton asked her guest if she had had a restful night. She replied that she could not sleep owing to a light under the bedroom door. After investigation she found there was no light left on in the corridor, and no obvious reason for the light. Mrs. Corbet Singleton replied that it was the phantom of the little black boy who walked there with a lighted candle, and that there was nothing to be alarmed about!

Dean Hall played a significant part in the Civil War, and two Royalist officers were slain there during a skirmish in the dining room. The one, Colonel Congreve's last utterance was a prayer — "Lord, receive my soul"; the other, Captain Wigmore, with his dying breath, cursed those who were killing him, and from then onwards, no matter how the floorboards were scrubbed, bloodstains remained on the spot where the officers fell. Eventually, the floorboards were replaced, but a dark patch still appeared on them. The boards were planed, and the blood stains seemed to be defeated. But not so; even now, in that corner of the dining room, there are dark areas which appear on the floor.

With its connections with Flaxely Abbey over the centuries, it is hardly surprising that the ghost of a monk has been seen there. There is a secret oratory in the room which was once the library, and the figure of a white monk has been seen, either standing at the bottom of the stairs, or crossing the room. Although this figure has not been seen for about ten years or more, there is often a sensation of a presence in this room during the late evening.

One of the Brayne family disguised himself as a gardener at one time during the Civil War, and it is thought to be his phantom sweeping at eternal autumn leaves in the court yard and along the paths. Twenty years ago, at eleven thirty one starry winter's night, a misty figure was seen moving from

14

Sammy's yard, near the house, across the drive, and up the bank, whereupon it vanished. It was a very clear night, and although it was lit by both the moon and the headlights of a car, it was not an identifiable shape, merely a gray figure, shuffling along. No footsteps could be seen on the frosty grass, and no trace of it could be found. Three years ago, footsteps and an angry huffing and puffing woke someone sleeping in one of the bedrooms. Some unseen person strode up and down the room, paused at the window, then paced to the door, slamming it behind him or her. The door was not opened, however. The occupant of the room found the courage to search it, and the corridor, but nothing and nobody were around. The rest of the household slept peacefully. Occasionally, strange sounds are heard in this room — muffled footsteps and rustlings, but nothing as frightening as the noises that night. It is known that two brothers killed each other in a pistol duel in the dining room over the love of a woman; could the anger heard in the bedroom that night have been one of them preparing for the fight? Or was it Captain Wigmore, who did not die gracefully, and who is said to move around the house, still cursing his murderers, searching for vengeance?

Recently, while walking with his dog one evening, the owner saw an apparition slowly materialising outside the house, at what is known to be a haunted spot. The dog ran up to it, barking and growling, but before the ghost took on a definite shape, it faded. There are many areas in and around the house where the dog becomes worried and agitated. Poltergeist activity has increased of late. Rat poison put down in the cellars has mysteriously disappeared, only to reappear in the old garret, which was the servant's quarters years ago. Other objects have moved from one place to another without explanation. Perhaps the poltergeist is protesting against the general disturbance caused by visitors to the house, since its opening to the public.

* * * * * * *

At the Red House in Littledean is a ghost who never quite arrives for tea. Four or five times a year over the last ten years, Mr. and Mrs. Bramley have been taking an evening meal in the dining room when out of the window they have seen a man walk through the gate apparently without opening it, and then fade away. He is a tall, thin man, with a gaunt face, and wears a black tall hat with what appears to be a silvery trim and a wide brim. His jacket is black and tightly fitted; only the top half of him appears. He makes no sound at all, and they have only ever seen him through the dining room window. When they became used to him, they hurried out through the dining room and kitchen to greet him, but they have never been able to reach him before he disappeared. The Red House dates from Norman times, and the dining room in which they eat is panelled with the original dark oak, and has bullet holes in it dating from the Civil War. At one time Quakers used the house for meetings, and it is thought that the apparition may have belonged to that time. During the nineteenth century, the house became the village work-house. A man had been murdered and his body taken there. Two suspected murderers were lodged in the goal at the other end of the village. It was believed in those days that if the murderer touched the corpse of his victim it would bleed, and these two men were taken to the Red House to undergo this test. The corpse did not bleed, but what happened to the alleged murderers is not known.

But despite its turbulent and sometimes gory history, the Red House has a very happy atmosphere, and Mr. Bramley says that neither they, nor the children, nor the dogs have experienced anything unnatural or unfriendly in the house itself.

* * * * * * *

Unlike the Red House, Littledean House Hotel has areas which are distinctly unfriendly and cold. In the oldest part of the house is a landing called 'Fred's Landing', where, no matter how hot the day, it remains like an icebox. Maids, guests, it doesn't matter who you are, the same hostile reception awaits you there. People have complained of

16

being shoved down the steps, of feeling crowded in as they walk along the corridor leading from the landing and of feeling forced to press against the wall to allow something to pass by, though there is no one there. A few years ago, a teacher staying in that particular part of the hotel opened a toilet door to see someone already standing there. With profuse apologies he hurried away, but had only taken a few steps when he realised that the man he had seen was dressed rather oddly. He wore a large velvet cap and a long black cape. Knowing that whoever was in there had not come out, he retraced his steps, knocked on the door, and when there was no reply, gingerly pushed it open. There was no one in there, and there was no other exit than the door itself. The house dates from the early seventeenth century, and was originally a row of cottages. Added to over the years, it is now a very large and welcoming place — except for Fred's landing, which no one can explain.

* * * * * * *

Often, children have gathered in the ruined Littledean Grange after dark, waiting around a smouldering fire for the ghosts of which they'd heard their fathers and grandfathers tell. Mysterious noises were heard, unexplained shadows and shapes seen, but most frightening of all was the white mist which would suddenly appear, sometimes hovering a few feet above the ground, sometimes creeping over the walls. A few stones covered by weeds and a dry pool are all that remain of the Grange since its demolition in April, 1962. But a man, now in his thirties, described to me how he and his gang of school friends were trying to get a fire started one night in the Grange.

"We were busy blowing away on some dry leaves and paper, when one of us cried out, 'Look at that!' We all stood transfixed as a thin white mist crept across the ground towards us. None of us moved as it stopped directly in front of us, then glided over our heads, slid halfway up a wall, hovered, then melted through it. There was no fog around that night; it was perfectly clear. But it was freezing. We all raced home, terrified out of our wits, and told everybody we knew about our ghost. Of course, we all said we had run home because of the cold. But none of us were prepared to wait for the thing to reappear. We never went near the place at night again."

Mrs. Smith of Cinderford sent me the following poem concerning the Grange ghost. The Gaafer Smithers mentioned in it is her grandfather.

GRANGE GHOST

Old Garge im zed to I wun day;
"Dick, near The Grange I herd um zay
There cums a spook by pale moonlight,
Me Grancher zidun thir wun night,
A walking drou them vields around
Wi out the leastest bit a zound.
Nu year, zays I, ther bent zuch things.
Ther be, im zed, thic un had wings,
Hazy like and mighty large,
Thay do zay zo, as my name's Garge.
But Zurry I'm zure we're quite wrong,
Fer ghosts an spirits don't belong
To these yer earth, but us two zed
Thick night us oodn't goo ta bed
But off to Littledean wood goo and zee
The things our mates could swear
Thir wern't no ghosts a haunting ther.
We tramped along the lane
A talking big an right as rain.
Garge laft: I be ready fer the vun
And down I squat upon a stwun
An put his yud between his knees
Fer I zaw The Grange among the trees
And out I got my bacca tin
An did begin ta smoke an pass away the time
Till twelve struck clear on Newnham chimes
An then we zaw a vloating ther
A hoss rise in the air,
Wi a white ooman on his back,

He was a skerry looking hack,
A breathing vlames as red as vire
An every step a galloped higher
Then a turned an come strat ver we
An Garge im did'n waat ta zee
What came of I, but took his hook
While I like a leaf shook.
I hollard doosn't goo but waat.
Garge im bunked an jumped right oer thick gate
And landed in a black tharn hedge,
Then did a nose dive in the sedge
An oer thick wall I went like vly
As if I were too young ta die,
An Garge when im had scrambled out,
Began ta hollar, scream an shout:
It wern't I who stole ole Gaafer Smithers load o coal
An us two run wiv vlying feet
Til we was zafe in Zilver Ztreet.

Anon.

And more.....

Just a few miles from Littledean lies Guns Mills, where guns were made from local iron four hundred years ago. It was a tiny industrial area then; in 1629 six hundred and ten guns were made for Holland. There are only a couple of cottages there now, but thirty years ago both mills were still standing, plus the pond and water wheels which powered them. At that time the Roberts family lived in one of the cottages at the end of the lane, near St. Anthony's Well, and one dark night, as he was hurrying home from work down the narrow lane, Mr. Edward Roberts was pushed harshly to one side, and fell against the bank. He turned sharply to give whoever it was a piece of his mind, but all he saw was a large black, bent shape, carrying what looked like a sack on its back, walk through the hedge on some path long gone. He ran the rest of the way home.

* * * * * * *

On top of a hill near a small village stands an old house, now used as a hospital for the elderly. It was built by a man called Harold Smith, who arrived penniless from Scotland and eventually became so wealthy that he was able to build this house, lining it totally with oak panels, and to erect several factories around the village. He married and had five children, but his wife became so ill that she spent the last years of her short life living downstairs. I talked to the grandaughter of Harold Smith, who works at the hospital, and she described how her grandmother haunts the house. Her figure, a lady in a grey dress, has been seen silently floating from one ward to another downstairs. She has an unpleasant habit of waking up some of the patients by blowing on their faces. Now that her spirit is no longer bound by her body, Mrs. Smith roams all over the house, especially the attic, an area which she had been unable to use for many years. The nurses refuse to go upstairs without a companion into the store rooms in the attic, because Mrs. Smith can be unfriendly at times. She will run up behind them and push them into cupboards or downstairs, or playfully tap them on the shoulder. There is a turning in the stairs on the way up to the attic, and Mrs. Smith is often here, either as a shadowy figure, or her presence felt as icy air. Her grandaughter has seen her here, "I recognised her from the photographs I've seen", she told me. "It is the only time that I have actually been face to face with her, though I have been aware of her presence many times. Seeing her close up like that was such a shock that I didn't have time to be frightened. All I remember is her calm, rather dull eyes staring at me as I passed her. It was only after I'd climbed a few more stairs that it dawned on me what I'd seen."

The appearance of Mrs. Smith in the wards themselves heralds a death at the hospital, which is why the staff prefer the hospital to remain anonymous.

The ghost in the garden of the hospital has an unhappy story behind it. Before the house became a hospital, it was used as a children's home. A little boy was running along the top of the garden wall sucking a pencil when he fell, and the pencil penetrated his mouth, killing him. One hot summer's day, a patient sitting quietly in the garden suddenly became hysterical, and pointed to the wall. She was plainly terrified, and because she had suffered from a stroke, could not speak very clearly. The only word that could be understood was 'boy'. She constantly gabbled out, boy, boy, and pointed to the wall. The patient was very sensible and kind, and popular with the staff and other patients alike. The effect on her of this sighting was very sad; she became quiet, disturbed, and morose, and would not go outside again. She died not long afterwards.

* * * * * *

A carriage and four has been seen careering wildly along the Bream Road out of Coleford. This vision has caused many a car to crash.

* * * * * *

21

Phantom Roundhead soldiers have driven visitors from their rooms at a guesthouse at Whitecliff over the years. The house was a billet during the Civil War.

* * * * * * *

Newland is also haunted by spectres from the Civil War; Cavaliers have been seen in and around the village. There are claims that they haunt the pub particularly, but the owners say they themselves have seen nothing. A ghostly coach with a beautiful lady peering anxiously out of the window has been seen dashing through the village.

* * * * * * *

On the Newland road from Redbrook lies Swan Pool, created to provide power for the iron smelting furnaces in the village. It is said that the cries of a child have been heard here, and the figure of a woman with a baby in her arms emerges from the water, covered with slime and dripping weeds. A large black dog then rushes out of the lime kilns in the wood, circles the pond once, then slinks back to its lair.

* * * * * * *

Ghosts of miners haunt the Forest as frequently as monks. The Pantod mine on top of Ruardean Hill is reputed to be haunted by an owner who was thrown down the shaft by angry colliers. This owner was said to be very mean, and refused time and time again to pay his overworked men their rightful wages. One night, they waited at the top of the shaft for him, quarrelled, and he was either pushed, or fell, down the mine. The colliers walked silently away, and left him there. Years later a bundle of rags and bones found in the mine were identified as his. His plaintiff cries are heard even now, on certain nights.

* * * * * * *

The Ham mine at Clearwell is haunted by an old miner who

diligently gets on with his work, no matter what. A television crew were making a documentary about the place a few years ago, and during one filming session deep in the mine, a man was seen walking across the set. He was ordered, none too politely, to get off, but to everyone's amazement, he carried on. One of the crew approached him, intending to forcibly remove him from the set, and the old man walked straight through him. In their haste to escape, much equipment was lost, and one man injured his hands quite badly.

This story circulated around the area, and some of the workers at Rank Xerox at Mitcheldean decided to go and investigate for themselves. "We went down the Ham mine at about six o' clock one winter's evening," one of them, who lives at Ruardean told me. "We were armed with a camera, just in case, even though ghosts are known to be camera shy. It was all a laugh really, though when we got right into the mine it wasn't quite so funny. We ended up about two hundred yards into the mine, down two or three levels of workings. We were settling down, ready to wait, when my friend with the camera shouted, "It's true, it's true!" He backed away and fell over. I looked up and saw an orangey glow in the back of the cave. It came slowly towards us, and it appeared to be a shadowy figure carrying a light. The light flickered, like a candle. The figure passed across the cavern, a distance of about twenty yards, I suppose; I heard two or three chinks on the rock, as if the figure was chipping at it, and then the man faded. It all happened very quickly, and we were all so terrified, that we ended up tripping over each other, and the camera equipment was smashed. Not that we'd tried to take a photograph anyway, we were so taken aback. We scrambled out as quickly as we could, and when we had calmed down enough to talk about it, we discussed with each other what we had seen. One of us had gone further on into the workings than the others and he had only looked our way when he heard all the commotion that we made. All he saw was a glow. But one of the others said what he saw was a light coming towards us, and a solid figure of a man behind it. He also heard the chinks on the wall. The fourth person with us saw a light becoming brighter as it neared us, and quite clearly behind it was a man with an old pick axe in his hand. In the other hand he carried a stick with a candle on it. He also heard the chipping on the wall, and saw the figure fade. We had all seen the same thing, but from different angles. Later on, consoling ourselves in the local, we were talking about the ghost, feeling a bit silly, when the barmaid informed us that he was well known locally, and the electrician who'd wired up the caves for the television crew had seen him often, and talked about him as a friend, though he added that the miner seemed far from happy. Whether the old man had been killed in the mines, or if he liked his job so much that he couldn't give it up, I don't know. I've been down a couple of times since, but not seen him again."

* * * * * * *

A bad tempered miner haunts the Baden Watkins car park near Clearwell. It is a commercial park, and has an old horse-drawn tramroad running along the back of it. A lorry driver encountered him one cold winter's night. He parked his mini there, because on that particular night he wanted to be somewhere which was peaceful and secluded. He sat in the car, and during that time heard or sensed nothing unusual. When he arrived home, however, he saw that his clothes were covered in sooty bootmarks. He couldn't understand this at all, and decided to look in his car. Inside it he found a line of footprints leading from the front of the car, over the roof, right to the back of the car. He told his workmates about it the next day, and heard how a miner had been killed by a truck on the tram line at the back of the park, and the park was known to be haunted by his spirit. The lorry driver had simply parked his car in the line of the miner's nightly walk. Another driver from the same firm parked his lorry there one night. As he got out of his vehicle, he felt a strong push on his shoulder, strong enough to make him fall over. He was in no mood for messing around, as it was a freezing cold night, so he turned round to tell his mate to stop fooling around. But there was no one there; his mate was still in the passenger seat. He felt his hair stand on end, though he wasn't a man to be frightened easily. He jumped into the driving seat and drove off, and had driven a mile or so before he stopped to close his door. No one parks in the Baden Watkin's car park on their own anymore — not the locals, anyway.

* * * * * * *

Coleford police station is built in the grounds of an old house. Police on night duty there complain about footsteps heard in the corridors when there is no one there. No matter how often the door to the interview room is left open, it is always closed when they return to it. The interview room is very unpopular with the work force there, and it is generally agreed that there is a very unpleasant feeling about the room. A ghostly motorbike has been heard to pull up outside the entrance, but it is never seen. The building is full of unexplained noises — doors being slammed, footsteps, creaks. No one can explain what is going on here.

* * * * * * *

Charlie is a very punctual ghost who haunts a house near Ruardean. At nine thirty every Monday morning he opens the kitchen door, walks through the sitting room, and goes upstairs.

"I began to notice Charlie when I was ironing," the resident of the house told me. "I thought at first that the catch on the door was faulty. It always sprang open and I would feel a cool breeze. I'd close the door and forget about it, but it happened without fail every Monday morning at the same time, and, no matter what the weather, I'd feel a gentle wind across my shoulders as if someone was walking by me. At times I'd feel the breeze on the stairs, and after a while, I realised Charlie's routine, and could follow him. I've never seen anything, except once. It was a kind of flitting across the mirror, a faint shadow. Very occasionally I'd sense that he'd paused behind me. I'd love him to materialise, but he never has. And suddenly, a few months ago, he stopped coming. For years I grew used to him coming in, and I miss him. The door remains well and truly shut, and either I've offended him, or he's finished whatever business he was about. I felt he was a kind spirit."

* * * * * * *

Gatcombe used to be an important port, as did a lot of the villages along the Severn. Sir Francis Drake used to live in a cottage here when he visited the Forest to collect timber for his ships. His ghost can sometimes be seen seated in an elbow chair within his chamber, gazing westward down the Severn.

* * * * * * *

About fifteen years ago, a husband and wife, who live in Bream, were driving along the road from Trow Green to Clearwell. They turned left at the crossroads towards Stow, and immediately the husband slammed on the brakes, nearly throwing them both through the windscreen. Standing in front of them in the middle of the road was a man carrying a shopping bag and a walking stick on his arm. Though they heard and felt no bump, they both knew that it was impossible not to have hit him. They both got out of the car, very shaken, expecting to find a body lying in the road. There was nothing. They searched the roadside , underneath the car, over the top of the hedges, but found no trace of anyone. They got back into the car, very shocked and speechless for a while. Then they discussed what they had seen, and both agreed it had been a tall, thin man, very pale faced, wearing a trilby hat, and carrying a long, flat shopping bag. The road is narrow, tall hedgerows either side; there was absolutely nowhere for anyone to hide. Many years ago, when the horse and trap was a common mode of transport in the Forest, a trap turned over at the crossroads, and the passenger was killed. Perhaps this explains the lonely man with his shopping bag, waiting at the crossroads.

* * * * * * *

At the side of the railway line at Lydbrook is an old house. A young girl who lived in this humble cottage fell in love with a man who worked on Colonel Vaughn's estate. This young man thought that he was far too good for the miner's daughter, and in her desperation the girl threw herself out of a window, and killed herself. This happened thirty years ago, and her ghost has been seen standing outside the cottage, with a look of sheer misery on her face.

Another cottager in Ruardean is plagued by footsteps running along floorboards which are not there. The floorboards were taken up years ago, and the floor is now just exposed beams, but still the footsteps run happily around the room.

* * * * * * *

A doctor who lives in Gloucester experienced the same thing. He spent many evenings with relatives who lived in a converted barn near Westbury on Severn. "At ten to nine every night," he said, "I'd hear light footsteps running across the ceiling and landing. The first time I heard it, I thought it was one of my relative's children out of bed. 'No', my niece told me, 'It happens at the same time every night. Next time you hear it, go up and have a look and you'll find the children tucked up in bed.' And I did, and they were always in bed, asleep. The footsteps were those of a child and though my relatives lived there for a few years, they never saw anything, just heard the running and skipping of what seemed a happy child. We all heard it, and probably would have missed it had it stopped."

* * * * * * *

A lady in a crinoline dress sits on the window seat at the top of the stairs in a large house on the outskirts of Westbury. She smiles, occasionally nods, and is only seen in the evening. She wears a beribboned hat and is very pretty. Sometimes only parts of her body materialise, but when all of her is seen, she appears to be dressed in grey.

* * * * * * *

One summer evening, while cycling home from work at Longhope, a resident of Shapridge Hill was generally admiring the scenery, when in a field near Abenhall Church he saw a huge building which looked like a mill. For many years he had cycled along this road, and was not prepared for the sudden appearance of a mill in what was usually an empty field. It took his attention off the road and in a few seconds he and his bike were in the hedge. He scrambled out, and, pulling himself together, looked again. The mill had vanished. Research proved that there had been a mill in that field, but it had been demolished in the nineteenth century.

* * * * * * *

A stunningly beautiful lady dressed in red and wearing a heavy perfume is said to haunt Clearwell Castle.

St. Briavels Castle also has its ghosts. A white lady and a man in armour walk around the buildings.

* * * * * * *

During the civil war, Goodrich castle was beseiged by Parliamentary forces under Colonel Birch, whose daughter Alice had fallen in love with a young Cavalier called Charles Clifford. She managed to join Charles in the beleaguered fortress, but the castle was forced to surrender. Charles and Alice attempted to escape through the Roundhead lines on horseback, but, trying to cross the swollen river, were drowned. Their shrieks can be heard above the noise of the rushing river on stormy nights.

* * * * * * *

If you happen to be driving or walking down St. Whites Road in Cinderford, don't be too disturbed if the white misty form of a lady accompanies you for a while. She founded a hermitage in the St. Whites area way before Cinderford was there, and people say she is a very kind woman, who seems to be oblivious to the busy road around her.

* * * * * * *

Yet another white lady haunts Hawkewell, but her history is unknown. She is thin and extremely beautiful, and her clothing has the appearance of expensive silk.

* * * * * * *

Mention The Coombs to any older resident of Coleford and they'll tell you tales of how they used to run past the place as a child because of the ghosts. It was a place you didn't go near at night, unless you were with someone else. The Coombs is a rambling Victorian house, now used as a residential home for the elderly. Isaiah Trotter, owner of Oakwood chemical works, lived there for most of the nineteenth century. He was a principal landowner in the area then, second only to the crown. A county magistrate, he cared a lot for the local community, and erected ten alms houses in 1889 on Berry Hill. He and his relatives were greatly respected around Coleford for their sense of public duty, but it could not be said that they had that much of a sense of humour or true compassion. This is what worried a female member of the family when she fell in love with one of the stableboys. She not only fell in love with him, but had an affair with him and became pregnant. There was no possibility whatever of her being allowed to marry the stableboy, and the shame she brought upon her family was unbearable. She could see only one way out, and one night she hung herself in the stables. Her restless spirit has never left the house and grounds.

The Deputy Matron of the Coombs lives on an estate which was built in the grounds of the old house in the 1970's. As soon as they moved into their new house, the family began to hear odd noises. The front door rattled furiously, but no one would be there. They'd hear someone come in through the back door and walk through the kitchen, and again no one would be there. One afternoon, she came home from work and found the front door locked and bolted.

"I thought I heard you come up the path and open the door," her frightened son told her, when she managed to persuade him to open up. "I heard voices, and I thought you were bringing some friends in. There was a lot of laughter and talking; it stopped at our door, and someone tried to get in. They rattled the door, but when I opened it, thinking it was you, there was no one there. All the chatter suddenly stopped, and there was an eerie silence." This happened early in the evening, but most of the noises occurred at night. On several occasions the whole family were sitting in the lounge when they all heard the door open and ghostly footsteps in the house. Gradually, they became used to the noises, though her son was so nervous that he refused to be left alone. The milkman knocked at the door one morning, and asked them if they had ghosts in the house. He had been leaving the milk on the doorstep when a white figure rushed in front of him and vanished. His dog cowered against the wall and growled and nothing would make the animal walk up the drive of the house again. Eventually, they had to dig up an old tree at the back of their house. They found foundations under the tree, which turned out to be the stables belonging to the old house. "I came to the conclusion that our house was built on the path Miss Trotter took to visit her stable boy," the Deptuy Matron told me, "And we heard her on her way to meet him. Perhaps the happy laughter and chatter belonged to both of them, and we were inadvertent eavesdroppers."

In the old house itself, the residents and staff have heard strange noises. "One night there was a bloodcurdling scream," a member of the staff told me. "It's something I wouldn't want to hear again. It began at the bottom of the stairwell and seemed to fill the whole house." Another member of the staff saw the figure of a woman in a long grey dress walk from the landing into a bedroom. She went into the bedroom to make sure the patient was alright, but found her deeply asleep in bed, and the room empty otherwise. "I wish I'd taken more notice of the woman," she said. "I just assumed it was the occupant returning to her room, and it was quite a shock to find that she hadn't been out of bed."

The ghost of Miss Trotter has many moods. She screams, she laughs, she chatters, she enjoys playing jokes. There is one particular room in the house where the staff hang their clothes and generally get ready for work. Here she loves to creep up behind them and push them, and to dunk their heads into the water when they are washing their faces. It is a room which isn't all that popular with the staff. A visitor to the house one snowy day heard footsteps crunching the snow behind her, but when she turned round there was no one there. Not only that, there were no footprints either, except her own. Then snowballs were hurled at her from out of thin air, and she was so terrified that she ran the rest of the way to the house. It took several cups of strong sweet tea to get her to confess to them all why she was so upset.

"In 1974, we felled another of the large trees in the garden which had originally belonged to the house," the Deputy Matron said, "And from then onwards we heard no more from Miss Trotter in our house." But she still haunts The Coombs, though less frequently as time goes on.

* * * * * * *

On the Whitecroft to Lydney road, a woman dressed in black has been seen pushing a pushchair across the path of oncoming traffic. Much to the consternation of travellers, she always fades before she reaches the other side.

* * * * * * *

It is well known that animals see or sense things which humans cannot. No animal, be it dog, horse, or sheep will go into the corner of the field belonging to the Rectory at the Forest Church.

* * * * * * *

Mr. Bolter was driving home to Coleford from Cinderford one wet night. As he passed Waterloo Screens, a car drove towards him, and lit by the headlights of both cars were two figures crossing the road. One was a tall man, and he held the hand of a small boy. Both cars slowed down to allow the couple to cross the road safely, but the figures vanished before they reached the other side. Talking in the Courtfield Arms; later on that night, he heard the tale of how, twenty years ago, a man and boy were killed on that spot by a horse and cart.

* * * * * * *

A woman, thin, and dressed in white, can be seen gliding around Wigpool pond. She is thought to be the phantom of a woman who drowned herself in the pool, though the story behind the suicide seems to be forgotten.

* * * * * * *

An inhabitant of Yorkley was leaning on her garden gate one summer's day, when she was startled by a friend of hers running towards her.

"It's terrible about old George, isn't it!" he gasped.

"He seems alright to me," she replied. "He came down the hill as usual a few minutes ago to have his nightly chat with me."

Her friend paled.

"He couldn't have done," he said quietly. "He was found by the milkman this morning. He hung hinself from a beam in the kitchen."

* * * * * * *

Foresters love their gardens, and on fine days are usually to be found pottering around in them, or leaning on the wall, ready to chat to passers by. A cottager near Cinderford always made sure he was outside when the shift changed at a nearby pit. He liked to nod to the miners as they trudged home from a hard day's work at the pit face. One day, one of the miners walked by and nodded as he normally did, but the odd thing was that he was an hour or so earlier than usual, and he was on his own. Later on, some of the other miners stopped as they neared him, and with grim faces told him that there had been a pitfall a few hours ago, and three of the men had been killed.

"Well, I know old Charlie is alright," the cottager said. "He went by a couple of hours ago."

The expression on their faces told him that it was only the spirit of his friend he'd seen going home that day.

* * * * * * *